GREED

PARTS 8, 9, 11

DIANE WAKOSKI

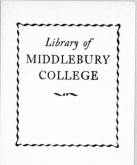

GREED/PARTS 8, 9, 11

DIANE WAKOSKI

BLACK SPARROW PRESS / LOS ANGELES / 1973

LIBRARY OF CONGRESS CATALOGING IN PUBLICATION DATA

Wakoski, Diane.
    Greed.

    Poems.
    CONTENTS: [1] Of polygamy.—[2] Of accord &
principle.—[3] The greed that is not greed.   [etc.]
    I. Title.
PS3573.A42G7   811'.5'4   68-4425
ISBN O-87685-156-1 (v. 8-9, 11)

C O N T E N T S

GREED/PART 8

The Darker Wishes—To A Machine Who Wishes To Be A Man
The Sad Beautiful Music Of The Poetry Robot

In the cover of his darkness,
his owl
a bird of purity and wisdom
sits in a white wood, speckled with the deep soft feathers of
perfection.
"Who, who am I?" he asks
in the voice of a singer,
in the voice of an ugly man who loves beauty,
in the voice of a man who has lost everything
      honor
      money
      his wife
      his children
      his mind
           even
in some deep wood
where only those with the eyes of snakes, who hold the broken wind
in their pockets
can survive.
This owl
with the cloak resembling leaves, twigs,
his beak and claws red from the meek animals he needs to live on,
and his amazing voice,
this owl pretends to speak in the language of men
asking profound questions,
but he is the bird of deception,
the bird of that saddest of all creations,
the intelligent machine,
so perfectly made he can long for only one thing;
the cliché of science fiction

9

and modern life,
he was programmed to do everything but make mistakes
and thus by definition
he is no man,
no poet,
no sufferer
in this common rapacious world.
Whatever he is
is different,
apart,
beautiful
perhaps
in its very
inhumanity.

Metaphors,
I kiss you goodbye
for a while
and will talk about my own perceptions,
angers,
and even the admiration I feel for the beautiful
scoundrel.

There is a waitress at the coffee shop of the
Holiday Inn in Corpus Christi, Texas, who if she
had not been born Mexican in a Southern town, near
the border, poor, and without ambition, would
have quite a different life.
Her hands are valentines serving my coffee. In
her face, reside the petals of oleander & azelia.
She walks like the wind in palm trees or a beauti-
ful woman's hair. But she will always serve coffee
to fat salesmen and dentists, and when she is fin-
ished talk to the short heavy Mexican bellhop. I
ask myself, often, about that Christian proposition,
"To those who have much, more shall be given; and
to those who have nothing, even that shall be taken
away."

I would uike to marry my Body-of-Christ waitress
to the singer of dark sad music, who uses the owl
to represent himself, and who has always walked
through the world whistling a golden piccolo that
disarms his listeners. I would like to give her
some of his luck and even things out, for I am al-
ways greedy to play god, but that is not what life
is about.
The Poetry Robot.
He says everything beautifully.
He says (and will sue me for quoting,
but they are such beautiful words I cannot resist)
    "I give up my heart which is a burning apple.
     I give up my arms which have wanted to leave me anyway."
and speaks of
    "the green field where cows burn like newsprint,"
and
    "The glass cloud in the shape of a heart,
     the owl arranging all of the night,
     the sleep of dresses on the warm bodies of women,
     the applauding wind."
His words have always been polished,
as if he pulled emeralds out of the mountains,
already cut and in Tiffany settings.
The natural jewel,
the naturally beautiful and perfect jewel-maker.
How we all admire his glitter.
And if we are wise,
we *will* admire the perfectly made products
of fine and sophisticated machines.

But pick and choose.
Robot or Man. Machine- or hand-made,
you cannot have both.
Greed, I keep reminding you,
is the failure to choose. The unwillingness to pick one thing over
another. Wealth or simplicity; you cannot have both. Accord,

agreement, harmonious relations with others or your honesty; you
cannot have both. The
telling of the truth
is not beautiful; does not make people feel good.
I do not think any alternative is absolutely right or wrong.
I do know that it is absolutely wrong not to commit yourself
to one alternative or the other.

And today I speak of this dark and handsome bird,
this singer of sad songs,
the Poetry Robot,
the mechanical Golden Nightingale
(but he comes in many other disguises, my friends),
because he is singing a new song this year,
stolen from another bird,
the song of his frailty and his humanity.

He sings the song of a man bereft of fortune.
I know singers with one eye,
men with no livers left in their bodies,
men who will never have women in their lives,
women whose children were given away to strangers,
black men who will not ever know the dignity of being taken
        for granted,
and those whose lives are spent in jail.
They are singers of sad desperate and beautiful songs,
not so perfectly made
but poignant in their human sacrifice and misery,
deep in their knowledge of life.
Their suffering sometimes carves out magnificent language,
but it is never the simple beautiful artful language of the Poetry
Robot, the man who cannot speak an ungraceful line.
But he has cheated us
and so I am complaining.

Surely art can be made from all forms of humanity.
Surely the golden song of the perfect man

12

is no less sweet
than the sad human voice of suffering.
How can you not know that,
you Robot programmed to know everything?

You fraud,
you golden boy who is good at everything,
whose handsome face has appeared in fashion ads,
whose wife is a sweet noble intelligent loving lover and friend,
whose children are gifted,
whose ability to make money will never be questioned,
whose speaking wins you friends in every place,
whose books will always be published,
you who can do what you decide to do at any given time,
you fraud,
singing now of having nothing,
of giving all away,
and saying your world is nothing. If your world is nothing, man,
then there is no world that is anything.
Be honest, don't
tell us that life is sad
even for those who do not feel. That is only talking.
Talk to us of the owl
who asks you questions in the night
and tell us of the long perfect nights when there is no fear or hurt
to invade them.
Do not apologize for your perfections
or lie about them—they fade as you do;
say you're sorry for what you do not possess:
      a sense of your own good fortune and the willingness to
      rejoice in it;
      an understanding that if you sense misery in the world
      others must be dying of it;
      your unwillingness to use that beautiful music to
      soothe the sick and the dying.

I met a woman this week,
who made me praise my own normalcies.
For her, speaking was like running through the blades of a windmill.
Her voice was like dragging a piece of metal under your car.
Her face contorted when she spoke
as if someone were electrocuting her for each syllable,
and when she ate, the food hung out over her mouth
moving like garbage in a river.
She walked as a bird would try to fly with a broken wing.
Yet she insisted on leading a real life,
going places,
talking to people,
writing poetry, longing for the language that falls cleanly out of you
like ripe plums off a tree.
Oh, you hypocrite,
don't you see that there is nothing noble in suffering?
That some suffering is every man's measure
and his only nobility comes from
seeing it through, living it out,
and transcending it; coming above it?
Do you think a man is noble for being beaten,
for starving,
for being unjustly persecuted,
for being physically tortured or losing everything he loves?
You, who have never suffered any of these things—
surely, you cannot be so foolish
as to wish to?
But the humanity of knowing the struggle
and any nobility that comes from surviving it,
that is what a mechanical bird cannot know.
My god, man,
you are privileged and above us.
We work
for what you have.
There may be a time when the world strikes you down too
and delivers no mercy.
Do not cultivate that time or long for it.

14

To do so is the opposite of what all life and religion
what philosophy and art
are about.
Sing
sing
sing
your perfect and harmonious songs.
Once you are honest about it,
even I with my torn body and painful memories
will listen.
It is the songs we want to hear after all.
And beauty is different, as each man finds it.
Give us your own,
tall handsome American and chrome.
Don't fall down,
or we'll kick you, where you lie.
Remember the fate of machines when they break down.
And we are always looking for new models.
Be yourself, #124966. And we will always
preserve you
for your integrity.

What is a philosopher?
　　　He is a man who gives no one the benefit of the doubt.

What is the artist?
　　　He gives us something beautiful from the darkness.

What is the failure?
　　　The man who cannot live his own destiny.

These are the concerns
of us all
as we struggle with our own failures
and deceits.

GREED/PART 9

Living from day to day is a series of compromises that must be made by every human being. To feel that in some way you are above having to bow down to those compromises is a kind of greed which often makes you long for death, which can be a kind of purity or relief from those human situations where you cannot always do as you believe, cannot have the life you believe is honest or correct or right; that to stay alive is to give up your standards or compromise them in exchange for life. In this poem, I try to address the destructive part of myself, a part I think every honest person has in himself, and to use the legend of Sylvia Plath, a poet who felt compelled to kill herself, as a symbol for that alter ego, that Diane who could not or might not feel that when her husband leaves her and the world does not honor her and she cannot have or do the things she wants to do with her life, that she might in desperation be forced to take her own life.

This poem is a protest against the deception of that sense of purity, that greed which does not allow us to accept life on its own terms and which makes us feel as if we cannot summon the strength to go on in the face of life's afflictions. We all have them, by the way, and I don't for a moment feel that this poem is in any way personal, tho it is written in the most personal terms. If there is anyone who has not felt these things, he is either dishonest with himself or has so far had such a charmed life that I would be loath to believe it were true.

I would like to say that I feel that many people will read this poem wrongly if they think I wrote it in order to talk about Sylvia Plath. I wanted to use her legend as a symbol and nothing more in the poem. I wanted to make a public statement that I feel she succumbed to a terrible temptation which faces us all; this does not lessen her work in any way but it does make her a symbol for the weak, the destructive, the alien purist in all of us which is not a viable product of human evolution. My poetry is an attempt to define the world in humanitarian terms; to embrace both the honest and the compassionate because it is love and truth together which will save us/ not love alone; certainly not truth alone. The poet, as everyman, must have them both. His vision must hold that greater reality.

In this poem, I wanted to do several things at once: to make a statement to the world that I would not ever kill myself, no matter how much of myself felt compromised by the world; to sing a song for love and beauty in the face of sad truth; and to make the male chauvinists of the world stop comparing me to Sylvia Plath—as if all women of the world who write well must be similar. I don't know that the reader ever has to honor the purposes of the writer, if for no other reason than that we seldom really know what we're doing when we are creating a poem—it being one of those dark and desperate journeys. But if you are a reader who cares about my reasons for writing the poem, then I am happy to have shared my sense of them. May the poem in some way speak for you too.

GREED / PART II

POWER

dedicated to C.B. who wants it so badly, and to all the astronomers
looking for new worlds, hoping to relieve us of one final fight
over this tiny foolish one

I am no expert
(tho I admire them)
on either owls or eagles,
powerful, big birds of prey,
heavy as mahogany tables,
sitting,
watching,
circling above the world,
waiting to see/ to capture/ to kill
what they want/ need.

> When something is bigger than you are, you do
> not argue with it. When man found all the other
> animals bigger than he was, he figured out how
> to be collectively bigger than they were.

These are obvious statements and bore me,
but power is obvious too,
and while the subject is not my favorite one, it is still one
on which I must discourse.
I choose to talk about owls, hawks & eagles,
because I really do not want to talk about men and women,
because I am tired of living with war,
because I am tired of struggling to keep my head free,
because I cannot stand to see the way humans treat each other,
because I am frightened of men who cannot control their lives
but who want to control mine,
because I am tired of receiving poison pen letters from a woman
who would like to rule my life,
because I am tired of being envied for a mythical power & freedom
others think I have,

because, simply because I have never tried to control anyone's life
and have often let others use me or push me around,
and I do want to talk about the birds,
rather than men,
because they are both innocent of conscience
& beyond redemption because of that innocence.
I want to talk about how much easier
my life would be
if I were the sun
and not the moon,
if I were a man, not a woman,
if I had no feelings, only desire,
if I were mercenary rather than compassionate,
if I were a gameplayer, not a humanist,
if I could stop loving you, whom I address these remarks to,
if I were an owl, or hawk, or eagle,
and my only voice were a harsh commanding cry
uttered when I killed some soft, fast-moving bloody animal
for a satisfactory meal.

But it is sunset, two days before a solar eclipse,
and summer,
in a warm place,
where I am alone,
especially alone—not even speaking the language of this country,
and I am thinking of you,
who are the sun,
tho your eyes are cold and remind me sometimes
of a snake,
though it just occurred to me
that they are sharp,
the eyes of a hunter or sportsman,
perhaps like those of a hawk or owl or eagle,
and for the first time in my life I am interested
in the idea of power,
if, in fact,
there could be a way to make you love me,

think of me,
care for me as I am fascinated by you.
But my mind wanders and is hungry for poetry,
hungry for an owl,
perhaps a barn owl, with its funny monkey face to look out of,
the infinite metaphor in its simplicity,
or for something I cannot describe,
something I call love,
yet love makes me restless,
reminds me of its terror as well as its joy.

What I want is life beyond imagination,
one that is its own
symbol, image and magic,
one that is music in a deaf world,
and I not a bird,
but for a change,
human . . .

There are those who do not believe
they can live their own lives without controlling others,
who fear that they might be dominated and ruled,
that tyranny might compel them to be sparrows rather than hawks,
but believe that if they ruled
the order of the world would improve.
But only with my mouth
am I a hawk,
a sharp powerful beak twists vowels into a bloody meal
every day while my hands are gentle, soft, cannot
hurt even when they are unjustly squeezed.
Oh, where do metaphors take us,
                                        not beyond description?
Do they allow us to say everything but what we feel,
do they twist our ideas and make them bigger than they are?
And the meal of language, pure food,
what strength does it give us,
dieters,

imbibers of rich edibles.

Power.
Men have power over women.
A simple fact.
One I have never come to terms with.

Power.
To have your face on the cover of *Time*.
To be in *Life*.
To be rich. To be loved.
Power.

Women have the power of seduction.
Therefore all our dreams of power are dreams of love.
My life has been spent looking desperately
for love.
My fantasies are of love.
I have a monolithic view of life—all of it based around
love.

FANTASIES OF POWER

Eloping With Bobby Fisher

Dear Bobby,
    I didnt come to Reykjavik this summer,
    because that climate is like
        a wound caused by a rusty nail,
        riding a motorcycle with bare legs,
        sleeping with a man I love who refuses to touch me,
        sitting, waiting, in a duck blind during pouring rain,
    and besides
    I didnt want to distract your attention,

knowing that the World Championship was important to you
and that my presence could distract you,
as the fox turns frantic
when he hears the black & tan coon hounds snuffing, panting &
barking on his trail.
You are not
a man to be seduced, I would think;
but hunted, yes,
as the solitary hunter and his fox or bear have a love affair
of ingenuity,
listening in the woods for each other,
seduction lost in the chase,
and yet the fascination of life and death gives all of us
killer
instincts when we are running,
either chasing or being chased.

       Alone
I could not help but think of you, retiring with me
to the bedroom
where chess games are not forgotten
but are played out between men and women.

I have always hated the
idea
that love between two people was a war or a game.
It is not,
in fact,
in the good life,
but
who of us
lives
the good life?
And this letter is my declaration
of battle with you
or at least the hunt,
a game of sport,

Bobby,
you are a challenge to all of us women

                                    can we prove
that sex
is more interesting than chess? You have ignored
us
too long,
and we are out to get you.
Right now. I'm telling you, Bobby,
that you will not be the only man in my life
until you yourself take a little interest in this game
for surely you know
that while I will exercise all my craft in hunting you
until you turn and pursue me
you will not win me, as a trophy.
Yes,
there is another World Championship up
for grabs,
the man who wins my undivided attention will be rare
and probably will have to resort to dramatic gestures
& psychological strategies.
Few have thot it a worthy tournament,
the arena of their affection being too tiny or trivial
for concentrated efforts
and I would not promote myself to any importance
either.
But game is game,
whether chess or flesh.
I could not seduce you
would pursue you instead.

Here are your competitors, Bobby,
the men I love:

First there is the King of Spain.
He has a gold tooth.
His footprints are often on the beach just at low tide

40

when I walk.
No one knows who my King of Spain is. I meet
him
wherever I travel,
usually near dawn,
seldom in bad weather,
he has studied the hermetic arts
and I have broken his pale narrow hand every time
he has tried to steal my heart.
He is descended from a noble family. Hunts only
with bow & arrow.

Then there is the motorcyclist & woodsman,
my betrayer,
the man who is dead & buried
but haunts my games
with the mask of an ancient bear.
I see him at truck stops.
His role is to paralyze me with fear,
to make me cry; he will help
any serious competitor
win the game from me.
He is the spirit of rice, fermented, reeking with power.

And then there is the truck driver.
Driving a baby-blue semi in his disguise.
And I?
What shall I be?
The woman's chess champion?
A lady mechanic?
A skydiver?
            A silent
movie star?
No, my disguise will be to be myself,
        small
        comfortable
        blonde

laughing
posturing
a writer of letters
driving a station wagon to deliver my children
to dancing school or fencing lessons
thinking about people
wearing a mask of scotch and soda
and so we will never get together.

Sex is everything and nothing, like food
or sleep; who of us
would live our lives for food or sleep or sex? And yet
we die
if they are missing.
I'm hungry and sleepy and horny now.
Remember I do not believe
I should have to fight for any of these things,
am sitting alone in a world whose walls are lined with books
alone in a galaxy full of exploding suns & dis-
integrating moons
alone in a sky where I've killed off an astronomer,
once one of your rivals, Bobby,
a solar physicist who read the newspaper
when we were in bed
and who quoted newsclippings for words of love,
a man who couldnt find
the north star,
Pole, polar star,
me with my Polish anger and revolutionary etudes in my blood.
A photographer
he caught me in yellow which I wore to honor
his province, the sun,
but I was a blurred negative in his camera,
just one of the planets or asteroids
which made a good picture.
No, Bobby, there's no competition there,
even tho I'm so lonely for a steady monogamous man

I could die.

And then there is the dean of narcissistic studies,
dean of men & women,
handsome with a red mustache & green freckled eyes,
his slim hips I would accept any night in the dark.
A man whose tongue I would cut out since it articulates
a weak voice,
a voice covered with baby powder,
expressing talcum views, smug insistence
and boring needs, oh
are there any boring human needs?
They are all ticks biting into our lives & burying
their pinchered suckers
into our damp skins,
dean, dean, dean,
not Jimmy Dean,
driving your Porsche into upstate New York nights
wearing a gold seal ring
on your little finger,
decaying into a moldy version of somebody else's past & future,
unlike the woodsman & astronomer,
you were really dead before I met you;
I did not even have a chance to kill you,
our love affair was practically necrophilia,
dead dean, dead dean,
dead man.

Then
there are the letter writers, Bobby,
the young men who are married
or love other women,
who all have mustaches
and want to write more than to fuck,
and I their perfect correspondent, the vivid
letter writer who's accepted
the pen instead of the sword or cock,

writing her letters to men she can dream of,
leaving a pale empty bed each morning
with one body's imprint,
since dreamlovers dont leave wrinkled or stained sheets.
At most
a crumpled letter folded under the pillow.

Where are the men,
Bobby,
who are not homosexuals or narcissicists
or playboys who make me think sex is trivial and dumb,
like fat women who make me want to swear off eating
for a year.
Where are the men
who come to the dinner table with women at night
rather than once a week in typed letters,
the fathers who stay home rather than sail the seas,
the brothers who love us without killing
themselves in remorse.
Are they all cold silent George Washingtons
or angry frustrated Beethovens,
astronomers only interested in stars,
deans, dead and invented, behind handsome mustaches,
truck drivers
who drive away,
motorcyclists betraying us small un-easy riders,
homosexual cowboys sleeping with their horses & fighting in bars,
chessmasters
who sleep with their queens before they are mated
and checked
and then never sleep at all
in the quest for the game.

Bobby, you see,
I dont even want to seduce you any more.
How could I want something so impossible.
I hate myself for these needs

44

and my own loneliness and anger at a world
I lament.
All the good men
are already-married men
and I envy the wives of close husbands until I realize
they think I'm a fool,
and that they envy my freedom
and the excitement of the hunt.
What can I say?
that we are all powerless,
all helpless and in pain,
all looking for love in an impossible shape
      for me, the sun blazing over water,
      for others, the cool moon, like an opal, egg-sized,
        in the palm,
      for some, a star which is distant & slightly mysterious,
      and others,
           the rings of Saturn turn dazzlingly
           like wedding bands of meteor stone,
    and for all of us, the hope of life,
    beyond ourselves,
    the power
    to breathe life into an image,
    which only appears now on a sophisticated screen.

THE PARABLE OF POWER

Let me return from men to birds,
I have no power over them either.
Stories are all I have the power to tell.

Once there was a family of ospreys. There were 2 beautiful daugh-
ters in the family whom all the neighboring birds admired and many

45

of the men were in love with. One of the young osprey beauties was a terrible flirt, while the other was quite modest and innocent of anything but her love for playing the piano. Now, despite the fact that Skinnerians have taught pigeons to play the xylophone in order to prove that behavior is learned, the beautiful young osprey who played the piano was naturally gifted and unique among her family and friends, none of whom knew much about music. (Other than singing, of course, tho the larger birds can scarcely be thought to have songs and their voices are harsh and very loud.) She loved nothing so much as the hour each day when a piano mysteriously appeared on a cliff over the sea and remained there for her talented renderings. Bach, Chopin, Beethoven, Scarlatti, Brahms—all the classics bubbled forth when she attended the instrument. But her sister who was flirtatious and only concerned with how many men admired her, discovered that if she stood near the piano while her sister was playing, many male birds, attracted by the melodious sounds would fly down and perch nearby and that she could flirt with even more coyness and charm while her sister played a Mozart sonata or a Debussy impression. The male birds, hearing the beautiful music and seeing the lovely young osprey preening herself, would forget everything but their feelings of love and desire. And, at one time or another, during the daily playing of the piano, they all proposed marriage to the beautiful and flirtatious osprey sister.

However, one irony occurred. And that is that no osprey males ever came by for these happy hours and, actually, the flirtatious young lady osprey was only interested in marriage with one of her own kind. So she always shook her beautiful head and whispered no, in such a way however as to keep the male bird wondering how he might get her to say yes the next day. One bird, a horned grebe, came every day and watched the osprey playing the piano. He scarcely noticed her sister, the flirt. And of course the horned grebe fell in love with this strange osprey sister who could play the piano.

This scene occurred every day, with a tension that increased in all the participants. It was as if a membrane, like desire, was stretched over the whole scene and each day was pulled tighter until now, our

46

story reaches its climax—something *has* to happen. And it does. One afternoon, the piano does not appear. The osprey sister, beautiful, desperately waiting for her piano, the source of all pleasure and power for her, waits quietly, her nature being modest and undemanding. But, tho she is patient, nothing happens. For once, the piano does not appear. This is an exciting time for her sister, the flirt. Exciting because she is talking to all the birds who've gathered around and for the first time she sees among the crowd a young male osprey. He is handsome and quiet, with a large mustache, and it is obvious that he must drink bourbon, drive a sportscar, and hang out at one of the hippest bars in New York City. She is, at last, ready to fall in love. Ruffles her feathers, talks with animation to all her friends, is feeling the membrane of the day and its cumulative reality stretched tight over her body, tense with sexual possibilities.

Meanwhile, the horned grebe has gone over to speak to the piano-playing osprey sister whose piano has not appeared. She is sad but not yet in tears. She had never anticipated the possibility of the piano's not appearing, but now she understands this reality, knows it may never appear again, that in fact her whole life as she has conceived it may be over. This does not make her cry because it is too complete and intense a realization to allow anything but gradual recognition—a piecing together of feelings that tomorrow will become sadness or pain, which will cause sorrow, tears, shock, desperation. What the horned grebe says to the piano playing osprey is not heard by her, because just as he starts to speak, a bald eagle comes and asks if this is the group which is looking for the piano. When no one answers (as they are all afraid of the big bird) he asks his question again,

"Is this the group waiting for the piano?"

"Yes," says the horned grebe.

"Yes," says the flirtatious osprey sister (hoping the young male osprey hipster will notice her).

"Well," says the bald eagle, "I think your piano has fallen into the ocean and is about 200 feet under water."

The reactions of all the birds to this stunning announcement were just

47

about the same. Some flew off; others started to wander away; and the two young lady ospreys sat down to think about this development in their lives. It seemed that if the piano appeared magically each day, and disappeared just as magically, nothing surely could affect such magic. That if in fact the piano fell into the sea, surely it could magically rise out of the sea again. They did not know why these things happened, who controlled them, or what had started the appearance of the piano in the first place. However, they decided that whatever Power this might be, was the Power they must seek and appeal to, so that the young lady osprey's piano would come back. The male osprey was standing talking to the horned grebe in low tones, and they turned to the two beautiful ospreys and offered this plan for retrieving the piano. The osprey and the grebe knew of a large fishnet used by a group of local fishermen, and they thought they might gather about 100 birds together and go out and use the net to pull the piano up out of the ocean. The bald eagle thought that was possible too, so the men went off to gather up their cronies and to embark on the rescue mission.

However, the osprey sisters were conferring about the nature of the magic which must control the piano and which consequently was the only thing they felt could restore it. They remembered that the first time the piano had appeared there had been a full moon and they had been sitting in the trees watching it. They had wished something would happen to make their lives more exciting and not more than an hour later, the shape of the piano had shone in silhouette against the moon, and the next day the one osprey sister was practicing her scales. They decided the moon was perhaps responsible for the piano and decided to write her a letter requesting the return of the piano. This is the letter they wrote:

> *Dear Moon,*
> *We loved your piano and are sad without it. May we know why you have taken it away? And if there is any way we can get it back?*
>
> > *Sincerely,*
> > *The Osprey Sisters*

They put it in the mailbox and went to sleep.

In the meantime the male birds were assembling near the fishermen's net and getting ready to try to haul the piano up out of the sea. It was, indeed, as the bald eagle had said, 200 feet under water. When about 100 birds were assembled, they picked the net up in their beaks and flew with it to the spot where the piano was submerged. The diving birds then took corners of the net and dove under water with it, wrapping it around the piano, tho with difficulty as the piano was wedged into a deep sand bar and they had to keep diving down to dig parts of it out so that the net would fit underneath. They could see the job would take more than a day, so when the net was partially secured, in fatigue they all went to sleep for a few hours.

The next day, when the mail arrived, there was a letter addressed to the osprey sisters and the return address in the corner bore the imprint of the moon—a pale white stain, crescent shaped. The letter said:

Dear Osprey Sisters,
Only the men who love you have the power to retore your
piano. There is nothing I can do.
                                    With regrets,
                                    The Moon

The osprey sisters knew there were men who loved and cared about them, but they did not really think any of them had the strength to pull the piano out of the ocean. However, they went over to the place where all the action was, for the male birds were awake again and trying to complete the difficult task.

Now, those of you who read fables and parables know that I must have figured out some possible ending for this story, either to prove that love is all-powerful or to prove that it's not. Any of you readers who are used to Wakoski's stories are more likely to think that I will

49

give a long, meditative, not-very-story-like ending to the tale, which will turn out to be a discussion of ethics or morality. But I would like to surprise all the readers by ending this story in quite another way entirely. What if I invent a rowboat full of angry fishermen who come rowing up with the giant moon, like a great blow-fish, lying in the boat, breathing heavily like the belly of a caught fish, with gills hopelessly opening and closing, out of breath from having been chased through the sky by the fishermen and now hurt, bleeding scarlet drops against the pale face, and the fishermen dumping her into the ocean, ordering her to retrieve the big net so necessary to their occupation, and the moon bobbing and protesting she can do nothing, till she sinks into the water and lies sadly at the bottom of the sea. The birds have been frightened away. The osprey sisters cry on the shore. The fishermen cannot get back their net which is tangled impossibly around the grand piano. The birds have no language and fly off singly, wondering how they had believed in such an unreal scene. The fishermen cannot retrieve the moon either, because power is easily lost simply trying to exercise it. We now live in a dark world where we only imagine a moon, where love is irrelevant, and life projects are as easily scattered as a flock of birds. Concepts are random, risky as chaos. We hold the world together for small moments which add up to an hour of piano playing each day, flirtation while there's music, writing letters to the moon.

*Printed May 1973 in Santa Barbara for the
Black Sparrow Press by Noel Young. Design by
Barbara Martin. This edition is published
in paper wrappers; there are 250 hardcover
copies numbered & signed by the poet;
& 50 copies handbound in boards
by Earle Gray, signed & with an original
holograph poem by the poet.*

PHOTO: Thomas Victor

Diane Wakoski was born in California in 1937. Her published books, which give all the important information about her life, are *Coins & Coffins, Discrepancies and Apparitions, Greed: Parts 1 & 2, The George Washington Poems, Inside The Blood Factory, The Diamond Merchant, Thanking My Mother For Piano Lessons, Greed: Parts 3 & 4, The Moon Has A Complicated Geography, The Magellanic Clouds, The Lament Of The Lady Bank Dick, Greed: Parts 5-7, The Motorcycle Betrayal Poems,* and *Smudging.*